My Body Is a Temple

Written by George Bickerstaff

Illustrated by Keith Christensen

Bookcraft
Salt Lake City, Utah

Library of Congress Catalog Card Number: 78-72565
ISBN 0-88494-354-2

First Printing, 1978

Lithographed in the United States of America
PUBLISHERS PRESS
Salt Lake City, Utah

Peter remembered it on the way home. Examples. He couldn't think of any. But Paula would have. Even though she was a girl, she was pretty sharp. Perhaps that was because she was his twin sister.

Paula was doing handstands on the lawn, so Peter found the basketball and began shooting a few baskets. Not easy when you're only nine. He wished he was taller.

"Did you see any examples today, Paula?" he asked. Her upside-down face showed that she too had forgotten. "Oh, no!" she responded.

"Dad will ask us. . . ." They both started together.

And at dinner Daddy did ask. He always checked on family night assignments. This time he had taught them about Paul's words: "Ye are the temple of God." Daddy had told them: "Your body is a temple."

"Do the terrific twins have something to report?" he now asked. (Sometimes, for fun, it was "the terrible twins.") It did not take long to make their report.

"So you forgot? Well, at least you won't get mistaken for elephants and get put in the zoo."

So Daddy went quickly through it again. Our bodies, the temples meant for God's Spirit to live in, must be clean and pure to house that Spirit. The twins were to look for examples of things that would make that temple either better or worse. And that temple was really more than just the flesh-and-bone body. "I'll give you some clues," Daddy added. "First: You are what you eat. Second: You are what you think. Third: You are what you feel inside."

"But it's hard, Dad," Paula protested.

"It's not really," Mother said. "Examples are all around you — even now, at this moment." And she and Daddy smiled as they looked back and forth from the children to the plates on the table.

Five-year-old Jeff knocked his chair over in his haste to get to Mother. "What is it, Mommy?" he whispered.

Paula had it before Mother could reply. "I know! It's the vegetables — beans, peas, corn, potatoes, right?"

"Right. We all know we mustn't take tea, coffee, tobacco or alcohol, and there are other things too that are harmful. Some things are especially good for us, though — like these vegetables we're eating. But remember, not all that's sold to eat is good for the body."

"I know," said Peter. "Like spinach — it makes me sick." That brought the laugh he expected. He really knew spinach was good.

The twins did much better the next day. At breakfast they noticed Mother's home-ground whole wheat cereal served with honey and milk. (They knew this was much better for their bodies than the sugared cereals that came in pretty cartons.)

That afternoon they passed each other in the school corridor. "You know what!" said Peter. "I saw someone drinking a cola drink. That's got to be bad for your body, right?"

"Right. And at lunch I saw two or three kids throw away most of their lunch and then fill up on candy bars. Nice, but not good, as Dad would say."

After school, Peter's friend Jim came around on his bike. He wanted to ride Peter's bike and Peter let him; but when Peter asked for it back, Jim still went on riding it. "You can ride mine," he said. "I want my own," Peter insisted. His was the better bike. Soon there was an argument.

"If you don't give it back, I'll beat you up."

"I'd like to see you try."

No one beat anyone up, but the boys parted with a bad feeling.

“Feel better after that?” Dad was just inside the door when Peter went in. He was home early from work and had heard the argument.

“I’m okay,” Peter replied, though he didn’t sound like it. He felt a little better by dinner time, and afterwards he and Paula sat down to watch a TV show. They were surprised a little later when Dad came into the room, watched for a moment, and then turned off the TV set.

“Hey, Dad! What’s the matter? It was just getting interesting.”

“I’m sure it was, especially for the man those three crooks were beating up.”

“But it’s only a show, Dad.”

"I'll explain." Dad sat down between them and rumpled their hair. "Do you remember my second clue?"

"You are what you think." They both remembered.

"Right. What made Cain a murderer?"

"He killed his brother Abel."

"True, but wasn't he first a murderer in his mind and heart — when, with Satan's help, he planned to kill Abel?"

They both nodded. "I guess so."

“Then take Nephi. In obeying God and going back for the brass plates, didn’t he see with the eye of faith and think of himself as actually getting those plates, as commanded?”

Two more nods.

“So, then, you are, or you become, what you think — a murderer, a prophet, or somewhere in between. Think violence, through TV shows for example, and you will accept violence as normal and perhaps even act that way. Direct your thoughts to good things, and you will improve your mind and heart — and the condition of your temple.”

Daddy rose. “And now let’s go out and play ‘Knock Down Daddy.’ ” Peter and Paula jumped up immediately. Rough-housing with Daddy was always lots of fun.

On the way out, Daddy put his arm around Peter. He spoke softly. "Remember your argument with Jim? Hard words too come from wrong thoughts. And they can lead to hard actions — a fight, maybe. Not good for any temple, I would say." He squeezed Peter's shoulder. "What do you think you should do?"

"I guess I should tell Jim I'm sorry."

"That's good. Go and see him after our game."

He drew away. "Okay, let's go!" And the terrible twins piled on him, Jeff hanging on his legs to try to hold him down.

After prayer next morning, while they were all still kneeling, Daddy reminded the twins. "Watch for ways in which thoughts influence words and actions. I won't be home till late tonight, but Mother will tell me what you found out. And be sure to read the scriptures together, just as if I were here."

By this time the search for examples was getting exciting, something like a treasure hunt where the clues were just dropped anywhere and you had to be able to recognize them.

For Paula, the big clue today would not be pleasant. As she walked down the school steps on the way home, there stood Trixie, a girl a year or two older than her, whom she knew slightly. With her were two boys. “Hi, Paula,” she called out. “Want to come for a walk with us?”

“Where are you going?”

“Oh, nowhere special. We’re just going to have little fun. We’ve got some beer and some cigarettes, and — well, you know, we’ll just do a few neat things. We need another girl to make a foursome.”

“No, thanks,” said Paula. “I have to get home.”

"Oh, let her go home to Mommy," one of the boys sneered.

"Yes, she needs her Mommy." The other boy took up the attack. "Besides, she has homework to do and piano practice and all sorts of other neat things."

Paula flushed at these words. She started to stammer a reply but was interrupted by Trixie saying, "Look! Here comes Cindy. She'll go with us."

Obviously Cindy was willing, and the four moved off ahead of Paula along her route home. All the time they were giggling and pushing each other, and she could hear them using bad language too. Soon they went down a side street, then turned into an alley.

Paula felt sick inside. She thought of what her father had said: You are what you think. These young people had planned what they were now doing. Unless they changed, they would go on thinking themselves into more and more wrongdoing.

Even little Jeff was catching on to the search. At scripture reading that evening he said: "I think I've found another example. Reading scripture's good for us, isn't it?"

"Well, what do you twins think?" Mother let Peter respond.

"It must be good for our minds and spirits, so it helps our temples," he said.

Then they read together some of the Savior's words: "Treasure up in your minds continually the words of life." "I will impart unto you of my Spirit, which shall enlighten your mind, which shall fill your soul with joy." And as Mother quietly explained what these words meant, they all had a good feeling come over them — a feeling of peace, calm and happiness.

When Saturday morning came, the three children helped Daddy with the yard work, things like clipping the lawn edges while he mowed, and pulling weeds in the garden. "Where's Mr. Rogers this morning?" Paula asked. Their neighbor usually cut his lawn on Saturday morning too.

"He hurt his back yesterday," answered Daddy, "and can't work — perhaps for a week or two. How would it be if we did his yard work today?"

"Wow!" said Peter. "His yard's so big. There won't be time for us to go swimming."

"Well. . . ." Daddy paused. "I was thinking about Mr. Rogers. His wife can't do it, and they have no children in town. But . . . I guess you're right. We don't want to miss our usual swim."

The three children looked at each other. They really wanted that swim. But they liked their kind neighbors. After a few moments Paula spoke. "We can't just leave their grass to grow, and if we did Mrs. Rogers might hurt herself trying to get it all done. Suppose we work really fast and get our own and theirs done. Then we'd have time for just a short swim."

So that's what they did. And they felt very good inside. Daddy said this was because they had helped someone in need, as Jesus said we should. They knew then that this must be another "example" of how to build the "temple."

And somehow they all seemed to enjoy that short swim better than they did the long ones of other Saturdays.

The good feeling lasted all that day and into Sunday. Peter and Paula felt it in the church meetings, and especially while bearing their testimonies in testimony meeting. They felt it while visiting their grandparents, while writing in their journals, and in the other quiet activities of the day. In the evening, as they sat around the table, Peter said, "Why don't we write down some of the examples we've seen this week?"

"Hey, that's a good idea! And we could draw colored pictures of some of them, too." Paula was good at drawing.

"Okay, I'll write, you draw."

So that's what they did. Mother helped them now and then as she passed. This is what they wrote and drew.

YOU ARE WHAT YOU EAT (AND DRINK)- - - - - - SO FEED THE BODY WELL

Grains, vegetables, fruits, only a little meat. (No junk foods or drinks).

YOU ARE WHAT YOU THINK - - - - - - - SO FEED THE MIND WELL

Read scriptures and other good books. See only good shows, listen to only clean speech. Fill the mind with happy, clean thoughts (By doing this, crowd out thoughts that are unworthy of a child of God.)

YOU ARE WHAT YOU FEEL INSIDE - - SO FEED THE SPIRIT WELL

Do things you know are right and that bring a calm, peaceful feeling -- like praying, helping your neighbor, attending church, obeying parents, being honest, acting kindly.

(Don't argue or fight. Don't create bad feelings, because they drive away the Spirit.)

When they had finished, Daddy came along and looked at what they had done. “This is really good,” he said. “Now perhaps you would just want to add a few words at the bottom.” He suggested the words, and this is what they wrote:

Always remember

MY BODY IS A TEMPLE

I will keep it clean and wholesome as a place for the Spirit of the Lord to dwell in.